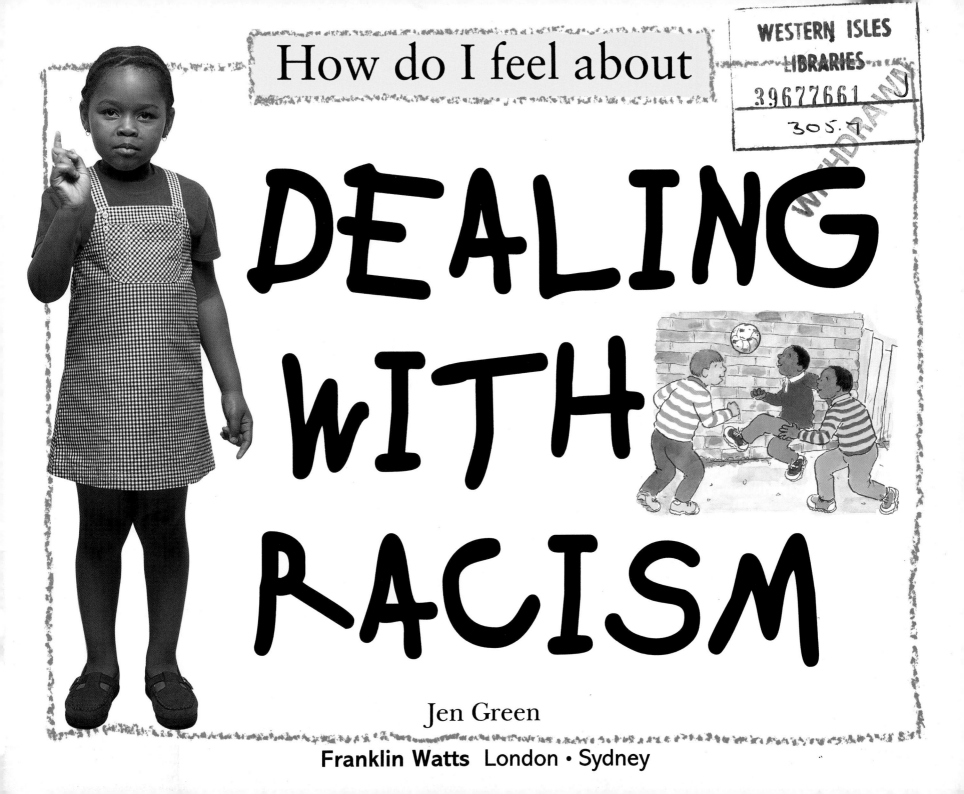

How do I feel about

DEALING WITH RACISM

Jen Green

Franklin Watts London • Sydney

An Aladdin Book

© Aladdin Books Ltd 1996

Designed and produced by
Aladdin Books Ltd
28 Percy Street
London W1P 0LD

First published in Great Britain
in 1996 by Franklin Watts
96 Leonard Street
London EC2A 4RH

ISBN: 0 7496 2559 7

A catalogue record for this
book is available from the
British Library.

Printed in Belgium

Designer   Tessa Barwick
Editor   Sarah Levete
Illustrator   Christopher
                O'Neill
Photographer   Roger Vlitos
Consultants   Angela Grunsell
                Rounke Williams

The author, Jen Green, has
written extensively for children.

Contents

Introduction

Raj, Pearl, Irina, Jo and Steve are in the same class. They come from different cultures or societies. They all get on well together. But a few people treat those from other cultures badly. This is racism. The five friends will share with you some ideas on how to deal with racism.

Racists miss out on many friendships.

We should be nice to each other.

Say "NO!" to racism.

Everyone's different—I think that's brilliant.

Racism can be really hurtful.

RAJ

PEARL

IRINA

JO

STEVE

What Is Racism?

Last week the class discussed racism. Jo said that racism is treating someone unfairly because of his or her culture – this means having a different religion or a different way of doing things. Pearl said that racism is also picking on someone because he or she comes from a different country or has a different skin colour.

Racism is being mean because a person's skin is a different colour.

When someone is rude about a person's culture, he or she is racist.

Racism can happen anywhere.

4

Racism causes unhappiness.

▶ *Name-calling*

There are different ways in which people may be racist. It is racist to call a person a rude name, or to bully someone just because he or she comes from a different culture or a different country.

*Out of my way, you *#/-**!*

Why's he always calling me names?

▲ *Judging Others*

We make lots of decisions every day. Deciding what you think about a person before you get to know him or her properly is called prejudice.

Racist people decide not to like someone just because of his or her skin colour, religion or culture, or even because of his or her clothes – without even knowing the person!

▼ *Why Can't I Play?*

Racism can be ignoring a person or leaving him or her out of a game, just because of the colour of a person's skin or his or her culture. Racists try to make others feel as if they don't belong.

I wish they'd let me join in.

5

1. The class was asked to bring food to share, for a picnic in the park.

2. Kim and Jane thought they knew all about the kind of food that Anu ate.

3. In fact, Anu brought pizza. Next time, she brought curry – they all loved it!

Kim and Jane were unfair to Anu.

Kim and Jane were prejudiced. They had fixed ideas about Anu, because of her culture. Racist people are prejudiced. They choose to dislike someone who is different, without getting to know him or her.

Kim and Jane felt they were better than Anu because her culture was different from theirs. This is racist. All cultures are equally special.

▼ *It's Not Funny*

Some racists make fun of the way other people talk, and then say they are just teasing.

But it's not teasing if someone ends up feeling hurt or left out. Racism is not funny.

◄ *Fixed Ideas*

It is racist to have fixed ideas about people from the same culture, even if those ideas seem good.

Each person is different. Everybody deserves to be treated as if he or she is special.

What do you know about racism, Jo?

"I'm Jewish. Last year there was a gang of bullies at school. One day they cornered me and asked me for money. When I said no, they started saying all Jews were mean. A teacher heard and put a stop to it. The bullies were prejudiced about Jewish people and had fixed ideas about me, without even knowing me."

History of Racism

Raj and Steve are reading a history book. The history of racism goes back a long way. For instance, hundreds of years ago, Europeans travelled to lands where people already lived. They claimed the lands as their own and were unfair to the people who lived there. Racism has affected many people in many different countries.

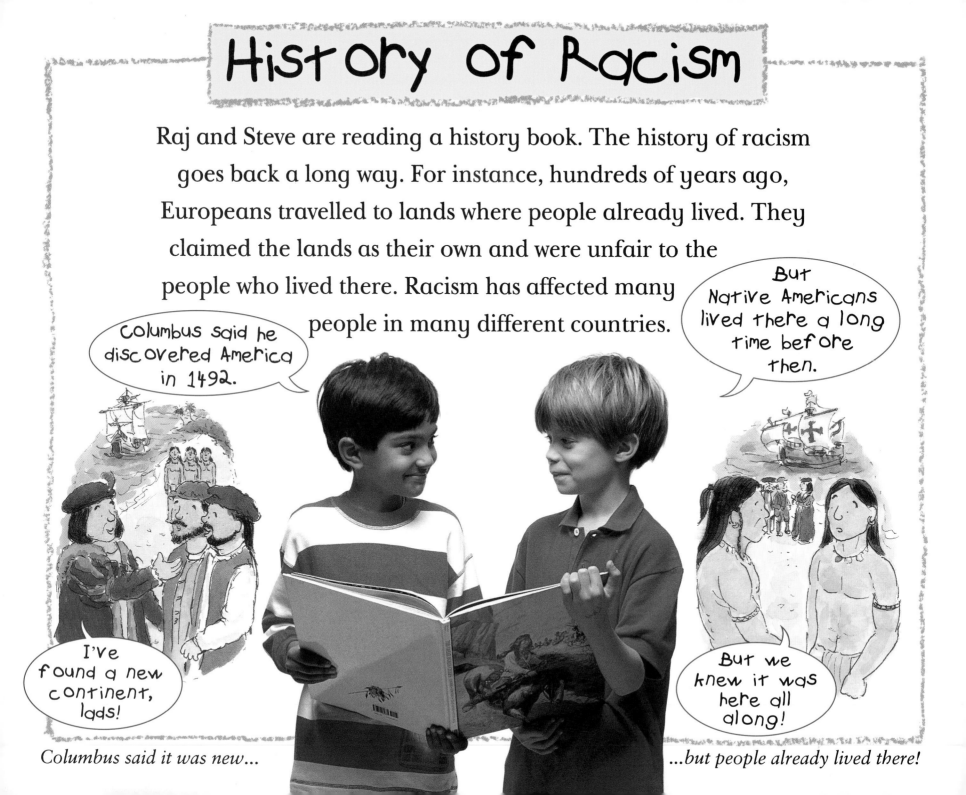

Columbus said he discovered America in 1492.

But Native Americans lived there a long time before then.

I've found a new continent, lads!

But we knew it was here all along!

Columbus said it was new...   *...but people already lived there!*

▼ Sam Is Jewish

Sam's grandparents were born in Germany. But when they were young, they had to leave because a very racist group, called the Nazis, began to attack Jews. Six million Jews were killed by the Nazis, just because they were Jewish. Sam is very proud to be Jewish.

◀ May's Family Is From Jamaica

One day, May wants to visit Jamaica where her parents first lived. Her great-great-grandparents were born in Africa. Europeans took them across the sea to Jamaica and made them work there as slaves. But all over the world, people of different races won the fight to end slavery.

Is Raj an Indian name?

"Yes. My grandparents came from Delhi, in India, but I was born here. Indian culture existed for thousands of years, long before British people went there. They treated Indians as if British culture was better than Indian culture. But I am proud of both my Indian and British cultures."

9

Racism Today

Steve and Irina are looking at a globe. Irina is showing Steve her country, Bosnia. Irina is a refugee. Refugees are people who are forced to leave their countries because of war or disaster. Many wars are caused by racists stirring up hatred between people.

1. Mike's big sister Jane did not like the Indian family across the road.

2. Jane was prejudiced about Indian people. She complained to Mike.

3. Later Mike repeated Jane's racist remarks to Rhunu. Rhunu was upset.

Why did Mike hurt Rhunu?

Mike repeated what Jane had said, without thinking. If he had thought about it, he would not have said unfair things. For Rhunu and the Indian family opposite, home is here. They have every right to be here.

Racist ideas are learnt from others. If friends or members of your family are racist, try to think for yourself. Tell them what you think.

◀ ▶ Green Or Yellow?

Racism divides people into groups based on culture or skin colour. Dividing people in this way is as silly as saying you can only play with others wearing the same colour shirt as you. But we all belong to one race – the HUMAN RACE!

Racism Is Always Wrong

Anyone can be racist, whatever his or her skin colour, religion or culture.

Sometimes people blame those from other cultures for problems in the world. This is unfair and not true. There is never any excuse for racism.

HEY!!

◀ Good News!

There is good news, too. In South Africa, white people tried to rule black people using racist laws, under a system called apartheid.

Now, President Mandela is trying to make sure that everybody is treated fairly.

▼ Unfair Treatment

A person may be stopped from getting a job or a place at school because of his or her skin colour or culture. This is racism.

It is against the law, but it can take a long time to change people's ideas.

◄ Gangs

It can be fun to be in a gang. But it is not fun if there are racist bullies in a gang.

Racist gangs sometimes attack people from different cultures or pick fights with other gangs.

Why didn't I get the job?

Steve, have you ever been in a gang?

"I was in Jake's gang. It was great at first but then some people in the gang started being nasty about Raj and my other Asian friends.

I didn't want to be nasty to Raj, but I was scared to tell Jake he was wrong. In the end, I told Jake what I thought of him. I left his gang. I'm really glad I did, and Raj is my good friend."

13

Feelings

Raj and Irina are talking about how it feels when someone is racist. Raj said when Jake picked on him, he lay awake at night, and had nightmares when he did fall asleep. Irina had to leave her country quickly because of the war there, caused by racists. When she first came here she felt lonely and sad.

How did racism make you feel?

Some people ignored me. I was upset and cross.

Racism makes you worry.

14

Racism makes you sad.

1. Paul and Ken were whispering. Tess heard them say racist things about Craig.

2. Later Tess told her mum what had happened at school. Tess was upset.

3. Tess didn't like what Paul had said, but felt too scared to speak up for Craig.

Why did Tess feel unsure?

Tess felt unhappy about the way Ken and Paul had acted, but felt too scared to say anything. It takes courage to speak out about something you feel is wrong.

If you notice someone being racist, try not to ignore it. Think how you feel when someone is rude to you and everyone else ignores the situation.

◄ Feeling Low

Racist jokes and comments are very upsetting. They can make you feel miserable and lonely. You might feel sick or find it hard to eat properly.

If racism happens at school, it might make you want to stay away from school.

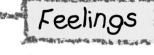

Not so good this week, Hiro.

► Keep Calm

Racism may make you feel angry. You might want to be racist too, or start a fight.

It's OK to feel angry, but fighting back is not the answer. It can get you into trouble and doesn't stop the racism. It is better to tell a grown-up you trust.

▲ It's Not Your Fault

If someone is racist to you, it can make you feel unhappy. It might be hard to concentrate at school.

But remember it is not your fault if someone is being racist. There is nothing wrong with you – it's the racist who is wrong.

▼ Feeling Strong

Racism can make you feel sad and unsure of yourself.
But try to remember all the things about yourself that you really like. Feeling good about yourself will help you to to deal with racist remarks.

◄ Talking It Over

If someone has been racist, it will help to talk about it to someone you trust.
Keeping your feelings to yourself won't help. Try talking to your best friend, your mum, dad, carer or a teacher.

Irina, how did racism affect you?

"When I arrived here, everything was very strange. I couldn't speak much English and some people in my class ignored me. I didn't understand why. I felt scared, and angry too – I hadn't done anything wrong.
Then I made friends with Pearl. Now I feel at home here."

Stopping Racism

Raj and Pearl are talking about how to deal with racism. Pearl says you could try ignoring people who are being racist. They might give up if they don't manage to upset you. Raj says he and Steve stood up to Jake, and that worked. But sometimes the best thing to do is to tell a grown-up.

1. Meera told her teacher that she was being bullied.

2. Mrs Bird knew where the gang played. She caught them bullying Meera.

3. Mrs Bird talked to the gang. They realised that they had been unkind.

Was Meera right to tell?

Yes. Sometimes you will need help to deal with racism. Tell a grown-up who you trust. He or she may be able to sort things out, without anyone knowing you have told.

If the first person you tell can't help, tell someone else. People who are being racist need to understand that their actions hurt other people. They need to be stopped.

Stopping Racism

1. Karl was German. Tim and Dave always teased him. This time Lee was there.

2. Lee stood up for Karl. He told Dave and Tim to leave Karl alone.

3. Karl was pleased that Lee had stood up for him.

Was Lee right to help Karl?

Yes. If you see someone being racist, try to help. Doing nothing is not the answer – it will look as if you agree with what the racists say. If people think they can get away with being racist, they will carry on.

If you are not sure how to deal with the problem on your own, ask a grown-up who will be able to help sort things out.

Racism Is Bad For Everyone!

Racists miss out on lots of fun and friends, just because they decide about people without getting to know them. If you take the trouble, you may find that you have lots in common with someone from a different culture.

Instead of being scared of differences, you can share and enjoy them! Every little effort that you make to stop racism will make a difference.

Pearl, what can be done about racism?

"My class discussed racism. We said what we thought. Some people were surprised to find out how upsetting it can be.

We all agreed not to let racism happen in our class. We said we would try to help if we saw anyone being racist. Now, when a new girl or boy arrives in our class we look after them and make them feel welcome."

Don't Forget . . .

Raj, how can you deal with racism?

"It's not easy, but there are things you can do. Try to keep calm. Think carefully about the situation. Sometimes, it's better to walk away. At other times it's best to tell a grown-up. Sometimes, you might be able to tell the racist to leave you alone. Try practising what you're going to say first."

Pearl and Irina, what do you think about racism?

"Racists miss out on lots of friendships, just because of their silly ideas about people.

We know it's hard, but try not to let racists make you feel unhappy. Tell your good friends how you feel. Good friends help you feel good."

How does your school deal with racism, Jo?

"Our school is very strict about racism. We all agreed that our school should be a safe place for everyone. We don't allow racism to carry on because it affects everyone, whatever his or her culture. We all have a right to feel happy."

Steve, is it right to tell a grown-up about racism?

"It's not telling tales to talk to a grown-up about racism. It's often the best thing to do, especially if you feel unsure about dealing with a difficult situation on your own.

Tell a teacher, a playground helper, your mum, dad or carer.

Racism is wrong. It's important that we all try to stop racism."

23

Index

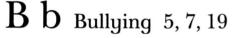

All the photographs in this book have been posed by models. The publishers would like to thank them all.

24